All About

Contents

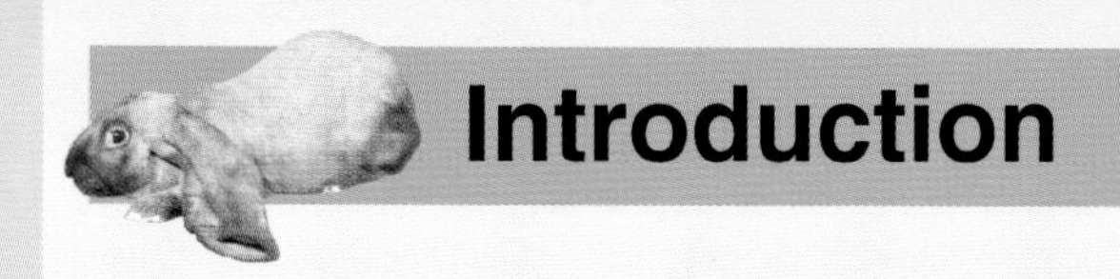

Introduction

Rabbits have been domesticated for more than 2,000 years, reared for their meat and fur. The Romans kept them in special walled enclosures called leporia. It was only in the late nineteenth century that we started to keep them as pets.

This book is aimed at the new owner of a rabbit who wants to find out how to care for their pet, and for those who already own one or more rabbits but would like to know more about them.

Is the rabbit a suitable pet for you?

Rabbits are now the most popular of all the small pet mammals. They have many advantages as far as the pet owner is concerned, including

- Low cost to purchase and maintain.
- Quiet.
- Hardy and able to survive in suitable outdoor housing.

However, there are some disadvantages:

- Low cost to purchase and maintain.
- Quiet.
- Hardy, and able to survive in suitable outdoor housing.

No, you're not seeing double! The very same characteristics that make rabbits such good pets also mean that they are very commonly neglected. Why is that?

Because rabbits are inexpensive to buy, there is a temptation to take them on as pets without thinking carefully about the care and attention that they will need throughout their lives. Because they are quiet and can be kept outdoors, it is all too easy to forget about them, particularly during the dark and cold winter months, at a time when they need more care rather than less.

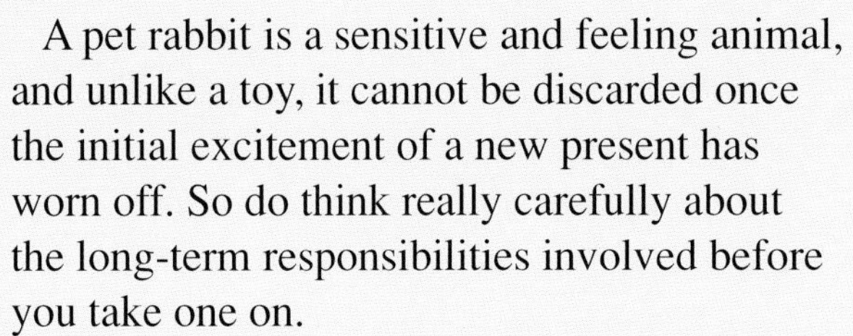

A pet rabbit is a sensitive and feeling animal, and unlike a toy, it cannot be discarded once the initial excitement of a new present has worn off. So do think really carefully about the long-term responsibilities involved before you take one on.

! Remember, rabbits move pretty quickly and can bite and scratch quite badly, so they are not ideal pets for young children, unless they are very closely supervised by an adult at all times.

DID YOU KNOW?

It is thought that the name *rabbit* comes from *robbe*—a medieval Dutch word for anyone called Robert. The word *bunny* comes from *bun*, which means *squirrel* in some parts of England.

Understanding Rabbits

DID YOU KNOW?

Some domestic rabbits change coat color depending on the outside temperature. Himalayan rabbits are pure white if it is above 84°F (28°C), but at lower temperatures, they develop their characteristic black paws, ear tips, and saddle marks.

Many of the small mammals kept as children's pets—such as hamsters and guinea pigs—are rodents, but rabbits are members of a different group of mammals called lagomorphs. A major difference is that the rabbit has two pairs of upper incisor (gnawing) teeth (although the second pair are very small), compared with the single pair that rodents possess. Like rodents, these teeth keep growing throughout life, and are kept chisel-sharp and at the correct length by the top and bottom sets wearing against each other.

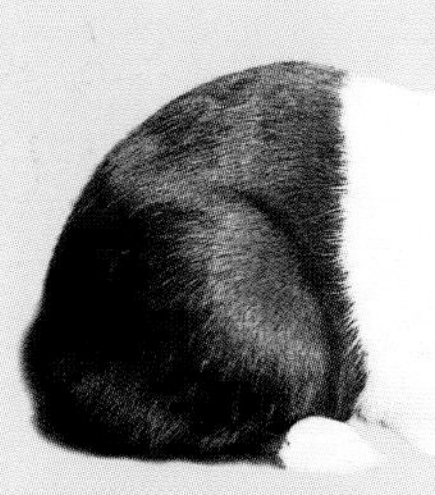

The enzymes that most animals have in their small intestines to digest food cannot break down the tough cellulose that makes up a large proportion of the coarse vegetable matter that rabbits eat. To get over this problem, the large bowel (the lower part of the intestines) is well developed and contains many special bacteria to digest the food.

Most of the digested food is passed in the feces at night, and these special, lighter-colored stools have to be re-eaten by the rabbit in the morning so that the digested nutrients can be absorbed from the small intestine a second time. So if you see your rabbit eating its feces for breakfast, its habits are not really as disgusting as they may seem.

DID YOU KNOW?

Whereas hares can reach 50 mph, rabbits are not very fast runners. Their strategy is to twist and turn rapidly to evade their pursuers while trying to find safety underground.

Buying a Rabbit

Most reputable pet shops sell rabbits, and the best will advise you on which type to buy. Otherwise, you may know someone locally who breeds rabbits and possibly competes at rabbit shows. Such a breeder would be able to give you all the advice you need. You might be able to find an address of a local rabbit club from your library or pet shop. You may also be able to acquire a rabbit from a friend who has bred some, or you can make inquiries at a reputable pet shop.

In all instances, look for a rabbit that is clean and well cared for. In a pet shop, it is a good sign if the staff are knowledgeable and can give advice when you are making your choice.

! Resist the temptation to buy a sickly rabbit just because you feel sorry for it—you could end up with a lot of heartache, trouble, and expense trying to get it well.

Select a young rabbit, at around six weeks of age, so that it grows up accustomed to plenty of handling and human contact.

DID YOU KNOW?

Rabbits really do breed like, well, like rabbits. The New Zealand White is among the most prolific, producing five or six litters a year with an average of ten young—that is 60 kids every year! Chewer, a Norfolk Star buck, fathered 40,000 offspring between 1968 and 1973.

Look for a clean, well-cared-for rabbit that appears lively and alert.

One Rabbit ...or Two?

It is nice to have more than one pet housed together to keep each other company, but rabbits do not always get along well together. This is especially true in the case of two male (buck) rabbits. They will almost always fight once they are sexually mature, and can inflict serious injuries on each other in the confines of a hutch.

Generally, rabbits do not always get along well, particularly if you try to house two bucks together.

A male and a female will generally get along like a house on fire, but they will produce lots and lots more rabbits unless steps are taken to prevent it.

Some people advocate keeping a rabbit and a guinea pig together, but guinea pigs are very timid and can easily be bullied by a rabbit. A female of one of the smaller breeds of rabbits would generally be the best choice to house with a guinea pig, but they must be introduced to each other at an early age and supervised closely.

The Signs of a Healthy Rabbit

A healthy rabbit should be alert and active during the daylight hours. Look for the following signs of good health:

DID YOU KNOW?

Rabbits can be trained to use a litter box indoors, and can even get used to being exercised on a leash if introduced to the experience at an early age.

DY CONDITION: *ll covered and nded. No normal swellings.*

BREATHING: *Quiet and regular. Should not be labored.*

EARS: *Ear flaps undamaged. No discharge or redness in the ear canals.*

EYES: *Bright and clear, without any discharge.*

NOSE: *Clean and free of discharge.*

COAT: *Well groomed. Should ot be soiled or matted, specially around the rear.*

MOUTH: *Incisors should not be overgrown. Dribbling can be a sign of problems.*

Handling a Rabbit

Rabbits are easily frightened and must be handled firmly but gently. They will occasionally bite, and will often inflict painful scratches by kicking out with their powerful legs. Rabbits should never be picked up by their ears. The best method is to grasp their ears and the scruff at the base of the ears with one hand, while the other arm cradles the rabbit's legs. If necessary, tuck the legs into your body to prevent kicking.

Rabbits should be transported in a top-opening cat carrier. You may need to put a light towel over a very nervous rabbit to calm it down so that it can be lifted out. If a rabbit needs to be restrained for examination or some other minor procedure, it will become passive if held on its back. If the ears and scruff are held in one hand, the rabbit can be turned over. With large rabbits, the hind legs can be controlled by tucking them under the arm of the same side, leaving the other hand free. If the rabbit is spoken to quietly and stroked under the chin, it becomes almost hypnotized and can be easily handled.

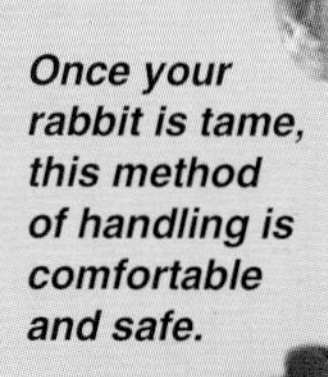

Once your rabbit is tame, this method of handling is comfortable and safe.

An Indoor Pet?

More and more people are realizing that you don't have to keep rabbits outdoors—they can make very fine indoor pets. Rabbits tend to use one area of their living quarters as a toilet area, so once you work out where that spot is, they will generally oblige if you put a litter box on that spot. Of course, they should still have a hutch where they can be kept out of harm's way at certain times.

The main problem with indoor rabbits is their tendency to chew things that they should not. For this reason, it is best to limit the rabbit to areas where it cannot do too much damage, and particularly where there are not any electric cables that it can get at. Providing your rabbit with plenty of safe chewing material will help.

DID YOU KNOW?

Lagomorphs such as the rabbit are more closely related to hoofed animals such as horses than to rodents.

Rabbit Breeds

DID YOU KNOW?

Rabbits took just fifty years to populate the whole of Australia after they were first introduced.

All breeds of pet rabbit have been bred from the one species of European Wild Rabbit, but there are now more than fifty breeds and about eighty varieties in a wide range of sizes, colors, and coat types that are divided into four main groups.

Rabbit Groups

Normal Fur

Normal fur includes breeds such as the Chinchilla, Havana, New Zealand, and Fox.

Rex

The Rex has a short, velvety coat about half an inch long, and includes the Self, Shaded, and Tan.

Satin (below): Rabbits belonging to this group have a flat, shiny coat.

Normal Fur: Havana

Satin

The Satin has a very flat, shiny coat in a wide range of colors such as Argent, Himalayan, and Opal.

Fancy Breed

Fancy Breeds include the long-coated Angora, the big-eared Lop, and the tiny Netherland Dwarf.

DID YOU KNOW?

The largest recorded litter of pet rabbits was twenty-four to a New Zealand White belonging to J. Filek in Nova Scotia, Canada, in 1978.

DID YOU KNOW?

The heaviest breed of rabbits are Flemish Giants, which regularly reach almost 25 lbs. (11.3 kg). In 1980 a five-month-old French Lop doe was weighed in at a Spanish show at over 26 lbs. (12 kg). The heaviest recorded wild rabbit was a mere 8 lbs. 4 oz. (3.74 kg), compared to an average of just 3.5 lbs. (1.58 kg).

The Best Pet Breeds

Here are just a few breeds of rabbit that make good pets:

Angora

Probably bred here in the seventeenth century, the Angora can yield up to two and a half pounds of wool a year. That's great if you're into knitting, but remember that all that dense, fluffy coat needs regular attention to prevent matting.

The Chinchilla: an attractive silver color

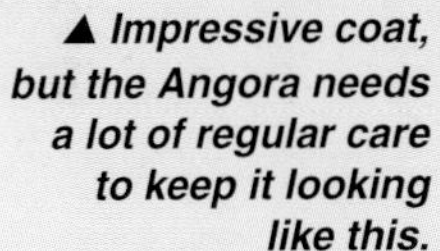

▲ *Impressive coat, but the Angora needs a lot of regular care to keep it looking like this.*

Chinchilla

With an attractive coat color that resembles that of the small rodent with the same name, Chinchillas used to be bred for their fur, but are now deservedly popular as pets.

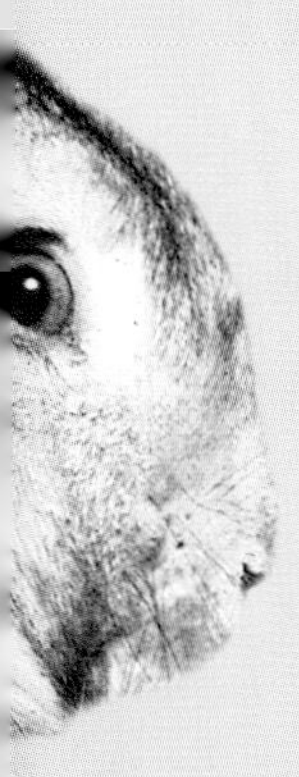

Dutch

The Dutch is one of the most popular breeds kept today. They were originally bred for their meat, but their relatively small size (around 5 lbs., or 2 kg, body weight) and their lively nature, make them excellent pets.

Himalayan

Himalayans have a white body and distinctive dark "points," rather like a Siamese cat. They are quite large rabbits, but generally have a very placid nature and are good with children.

Lops

There are several varieties of Lop rabbits, all with the distinctive "Dumbo" ears. The dwarf Lop is probably the most suitable as a pet, as it is generally sociable and not too large.

DID YOU KNOW?

The longest-eared rabbit is a black English Lop "Sweet Majestic Star," bred by Therese and Cheryl Seward of Exeter, Devon, England, with an ear span of 28.5 in. from tip to tip. An ear span of more than 30 in. was recorded in 1901, but this is thought to have been aided by stretching the ears with weights.

Netherland Dwarf

The Netherland Dwarf is very popular as a children's pet because of its small size, weighing only about 2 lbs. (1 kg). They require less living space than the larger breeds, but are not as sturdy and can sometimes be a little nervous. A smaller pet is not necessarily the best choice for a smaller person.

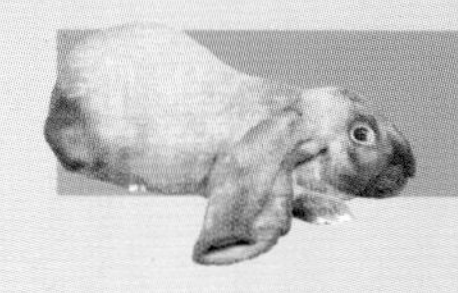

An Ideal Home

Size **A hutch measuring 3 ft wide, 2 ft deep and 2 ft high (90 x 60 x 60 cm) would be considered the minimum size. More space will be needed for the larger breeds.**

Well-insulated and sturdy construction

An outdoor hutch will need to be more sturdily constructed than one for indoor use. It should be made of marine plywood or suitably treated hardwood (but not on the inside). Waterproof roofing felt should be fitted to the top, sloping to the back, with an overhang at the front.

There should be two compartments divided by a partition with a sliding door. The larger compartment should have a wire-mesh front, and the smaller sleeping compartment should have a solid front to help keep the warmth in. Cleaning is easier if the compartments have removable metal or plastic litter boxes that can be slid out from the bottom of the hutch.

Raised off the ground

The hutch should be raised at least nine inches off the ground on legs to prevent dampness from penetrating. If it is attached to a run, a ramp will be needed so the rabbits can get in and out of the hutch.

Warmth

There is no need to provide extra heating even in winter, but it is essential that the hutch is waterproof and well insulated. Some heavy burlap on top of the cage will provide extra insulation, which can be pulled down over the front of the cage at night.

Living quarters with wire-mesh front

The wire mesh on the front of the cage needs to be fine enough to keep rats and mice from entering. The opening front panels must be secure when closed to prevent the rabbit from escaping, and to stop foxes from breaking in.

Bedding material

Rabbits produce a lot of urine and feces, so the cage will need cleaning every couple of days, with a more thorough spring clean about once a week. Provide your rabbit with plenty of clean and dry bedding material. Wood shavings, straw, or peat all make a good base, and rabbits do appreciate some hay, which can be eaten as well as being used for bedding.

Make sure you purchase hay or straw from a reputable source, and check to make sure it is clean, free from mold and not excessively dusty. Shredded paper is also available from pet supply stores, and this is a relatively mess-free alternative for indoor rabbits.

Other Equipment

DID YOU KNOW?

Some lengths of fairly wide drain piping are often appreciated in a rabbit's run and can be placed together to make a maze. This will provide shade and cater to the rabbit's instinct to live in tunnels.

FEEDING BOWL:
A ceramic bowl will be needed for dry food. This should be deep enough to keep the food clean and dry.

WATER-BOTTLE:
Water bottles with a valve on the spout at the bottom, which can be turned upside down, are most commonly used nowadays, as they keep the water cleaner than in a bowl. Ensure a supply of fresh water is always available, and check that the bottle does not leak water onto the bedding. In the depths of winter, you must check outdoor hutches regularly in case the water in the bottle has frozen.

Fresh water should always be available.

Run, Rabbit, Run...

An outdoor run will decrease the risk of rabbits escaping from the garden, and it will also stop them from nibbling at highly prized, or even poisonous, plants. The rabbits will be safe and secure, protected from predators, and they should be fairly easy to catch at night.

A simple run can be constructed from a softwood framework covered with wire mesh, taking great care to ensure there are no sharp ends protruding that could harm the rabbit. If you cover one end of the run with some translucent plastic, this will provide a shaded area; otherwise the run must be sited so that natural shade is provided on sunny days. Of course, the rabbits will need a water supply within the run.

As rabbits can dig very well, the run will be more secure if it has a wire-mesh base that is coarse enough to enable the rabbit to nibble at the grass underneath easily. The run can be moved around the lawn to give the rabbit new areas to graze on and to avoid damage to the grass. Do not allow a rabbit that has been over-wintered on hay to suddenly have unlimited access to fresh spring grass. Too much grass, eaten too quickly, may cause diarrhea.

Even if your rabbit is allowed freedom indoors, it will benefit from access to an outdoor run when possible.

Feeding Your Rabbit

Rabbits will eat a wide variety of vegetable matter, but it is best to base their diet upon a balanced food, such as that formulated in pellets for laboratory rabbits.

Many rabbits do very well on a complete food based on alfalfa. They enjoy hay, especially in winter, when they do not have access to fresh grass and boredom can be a problem. Lettuce has very little nutritional value, and too much can cause diarrhea, but sprouts, cabbage, carrots, cauliflower, peas (and their pods), rutabaga, and turnip are all appreciated.

DID YOU KNOW?

The rabbit's mouth contains 17,000 taste buds, compared with 10,000 in humans.

Resist the temptation to save money by buying prepared foods in large quantities if you have only one or two rabbits. If the food is stored for too long, it may lose some of its goodness, or it may spoil—especially in damp conditions.

Whole wheat bread that has been dried in the oven until hard will help to exercise your rabbit's teeth.

DID YOU KNOW?

Three rabbits will eat as much grass in a day as one sheep, making them a serious pest to farmers. Ferrets were bred from weasels to go down burrows and kill rabbits, but in some coastal regions, crabs and lobsters were sent down burrows to try to chase them out.

Dried food can be left in a bowl in the hutch for the rabbits to help themselves. However, succulent food must be removed from the hutch before it spoils.

getables such as bbage will be preciated.

Sexing Rabbits

DID YOU KNOW?

A pregnant doe will need twice as much food as normal by the end of her pregnancy, and three times normal while she is feeding her young.

Female rabbits are called does and males are called bucks. It is very easy to tell them apart as adults: the doe has a slit-like vaginal opening, whereas the buck has very obvious testicles, and the penis can be exposed by pulling back gently on the genital opening.

Sexing young rabbits is more difficult—even experts sometimes get it wrong! It is best to compare a male and a female side by side to see the difference. In the doe, the vaginal opening is more noticeably slit-like, and in the buck, there is greater distance from the anus to the genital opening. Although the testicles do not descend until the rabbit matures sexually, it is still possible to expose the penis in a young rabbit.

Family Planning for Rabbits

This is pretty important if you want to keep mixed-sex groups of rabbits together. Even if you allow your rabbits to breed, this must be limited as you will not be able to cope with the vast number of young that will be produced. Uncontrolled breeding is also likely to have an adverse effect on the does, resulting in a loss of condition.

Modern anesthetics are now much safer than they used to be, and although it must be accepted that rabbits are higher-risk patients than dogs and cats, surgical neutering is a viable option. Castration of male rabbits has been used for a long time to help reduce the aggressive tendencies that some bucks develop as they mature, but it is also possible to remove the ovaries and womb of female rabbits, just as in cats and dogs.

Doe rabbits can breed at any time of the year, as their ovaries produce eggs "to order," as a result of the act of mating with a buck. They can have several litters each year, with an average of five per litter, but it is not advisable to allow a pet doe to have more than three litters a year. The doe should be taken to the buck to see if she is ready to mate.

Pregnancy lasts about one month, and the pregnant doe will make a nest, lined with her own hair, ready for her litter. She will appreciate a shallow nesting box about 2 in. (6 cm) deep, lined with hay, in one corner of her sleeping compartment.

The young are generally born at night, and problems are rare. The doe should be watched from a distance, and veterinary assistance sought if she strains for more than an hour without producing any young.

Great care must be taken not to distress the doe or to handle her young before they emerge from the nest, as she may turn on them and kill them.

It is normal for her to eat the afterbirth, which is expelled after each baby.

Although the young are born very immature, they develop quickly:

Day 7
Fur growing

Day 10
Eyes open

Day 12
Ears open

Day 18
Leave the nest and eat solid food

Day 60 (2 months)
Fully weaned and independent

Day 150 (5 months)
Sexually mature and able to breed

DID YOU KNOW?

A rabbit's incisors (front teeth) can grow as much as 5 inches in one year.

Grooming

The amount of grooming your rabbit requires will depend if it is longhaired or shorthaired. Shorthaired rabbits do not need regular grooming, but when they are in heavy molt—usually once or twice a year—they will benefit from being brushed. A longhaired rabbit, such as a Cashmere Lop, will need grooming on a weekly basis, whereas the Angora needs thorough grooming several times a week.

Nails

Many rabbits go through their lives without ever needing their nails clipped, keeping them worn down by digging and hopping around on hard ground. However, if the nails are overgrowing, they can be cut back with nail clippers to about one-quarter of an inch (½ cm) from the end of the quick. It is easy to see where the pink, sensitive quick is in unpigmented nails, but this may be harder when the nails are colored. If a nail breaks accidentally or is cut too short, it may bleed profusely. This is uncomfortable for the rabbit, but there is no need to panic, because the bleeding soon stops.

Teeth

It is not unusual for a rabbit's teeth to get too long. It occurs if the teeth grow out of alignment and fail to wear against each other properly. This can cause a lot of discomfort, with the rabbit showing difficulty in eating, and possibly dribbling saliva down its chin. It is quite easy to see if the front teeth are overgrown, and a vet can cut them back. But overgrown back teeth are more difficult to see because the rabbit's mouth is small. A vet can use a lighted speculum to see the back teeth. If they need filing down, this will have to be done under anesthetic.

Vaccinations

Rabbits should be vaccinated against myxomatosis and viral hemorrhagic disease, both serious viral diseases that are usually fatal. As myxomatosis is spread by biting insects, even a rabbit that lives on its own can contract the disease. The vaccinations need boosting at least once a year, and this is a good opportunity for a regular health check.

Going Away

Rabbits should not be left unattended for long periods. If they are safely locked in a clean hutch with a supply of dry food and water, they should be fine for a couple of days. If you leave your rabbit for a longer period, try boarding it with a vet, a pet shop, or perhaps a breeder. If you have a good neighbor, a check once or twice a day for feeding and cleaning should be sufficient. Make sure that whoever looks after your rabbit knows all about its needs, and leave a number for your vet in case of problems.

Health Problems

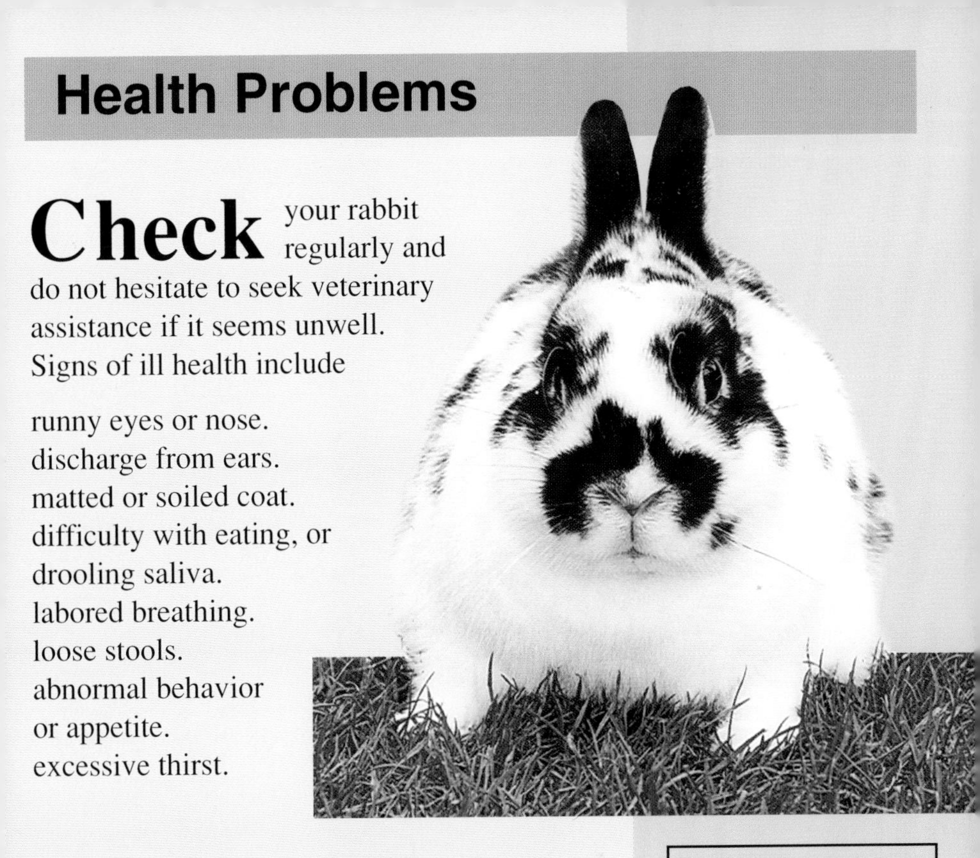

Check your rabbit regularly and do not hesitate to seek veterinary assistance if it seems unwell. Signs of ill health include

runny eyes or nose.
discharge from ears.
matted or soiled coat.
difficulty with eating, or drooling saliva.
labored breathing.
loose stools.
abnormal behavior or appetite.
excessive thirst.

Common Ailments

Snuffles

Respiratory infections are common in rabbits, especially if their housing is poorly ventilated. They can cause "snuffles" with a chronically snotty nose and noisy breathing. Although antibiotics can sometimes upset the natural balance of bacteria in the rabbit's bowel, this is a situation where they generally have to be used.

DID YOU KNOW?

The sense of smell is very important to a rabbit. It is used for seeking out food, sensing the approach of predators, and for identifying their territory. Male rabbits mark out their territory by spraying urine and by transferring scent from special glands under their chin onto their paws, and then stamping it along the borders of their patch.

Health Problems

Abscesses

Perhaps the most common problem of all in rabbits are abscesses filled with a thick, toothpasty pus caused by an organism called pastuerella. Small abscesses can be lanced and treated with antibiotics, but rabbits often get multiple ones that fail to respond to treatment.

Heatstroke

Rabbits are much more susceptible to the effects of excessive heat than from the cold. Make sure your rabbits have adequate shade in the summer and plenty of water to drink. If your rabbit seems weak or collapsed, and you think heatstroke may be the cause, sponge it down with cool water immediately to reduce its body temperature, and then seek veterinary help.

DID YOU KNOW?

Rabbits are color blind, but with their eyes set high up on either side of their head, they are able to see about 300 degrees of the full 360 degrees around them. In this way they can spot any predator stalking up behind them while they are grazing.

Fly Strike

All too often a consequence of diarrhea, flies will quickly gain a hold in hot weather when the skin is inflamed and soiled. Eggs are laid on the hairs, and the maggots that hatch out will eat into the flesh of the rabbit. This needs prompt treatment by a vet if the rabbit is to be saved. Good hygiene and regular examination of the rear area of the rabbit can prevent this problem.

Diarrhea

Diarrhea commonly is due to infections or parasitic problems, or sometimes simply a dietary problem. Providing a complete dry food and removing greenstuffs from the diet may do the trick in mild cases. Laboratory analysis of a feces sample may be needed to establish the diagnosis.

Fur Balls

Hair balls can build up in the stomach, causing a loss of appetite and distension of the abdomen. A 5 ml dose of liquid paraffin (mineral oil) may clear the problem, but sometimes surgical intervention is needed.

Poisoning

Anenome, autumn crocus, bluebells, elder, figwort, foxglove, poppy, nightshades, and wild clematis are all examples of plants that can be poisonous to rabbits. There are no specific antidotes to most poisonous plants, but, obviously, restrict access to any you think could be troublesome. Rabbits are generally pretty sensible about what they choose to eat, but if you rabbit is off-color, develops diarrhea, twitches, or even has convulsions, you should seek veterinary advice. Take along samples of any suspect plants your rabbit may have eaten.

DID YOU KNOW?

The normal life span of a rabbit is six to eight years. The oldest rabbit recorded was Flopsy, a wild rabbit caught on August 6, 1964 in Tasmania, that was kept as a pet and died in June 1983 at the age of nearly 18 years and 11 months.

If your rabbit is seriously ill, your veterinarian must be contacted for assistance without delay. In this case, a responsible adult will need to take the rabbit to the veterinarian and authorize any treatment that may be needed.

Most small animal veterinary practices see a large number of small mammals and are very willing and able to treat them. Nowadays it is not uncommon to anesthetize rabbits in order to carry out surgical operations such as tumor removal or draining large abscesses, although the risks are greater than for a cat or a dog undergoing a similar procedure.

!

The most important care for a sick or injured rabbit is to keep it warm and administer fluids to try to prevent dehydration, which can occur quite quickly. A dropper or a small syringe is ideal for administering solutions, but do not use excessive force, and remember that fluids can do more harm than good if they are inhaled.

Commercial rehydration powders that are designed to be made up with water can be purchased from a vet or a pharmacist, but a rabbit will take only a few drops at a time. Alternatively, you can use boiled tap water that has been allowed to cool, adding a heaping tablespoonful of glucose powder and a level teaspoonful of salt.

Small Wounds

Small wounds can be gently flushed with warm water and treated with a mild antiseptic, but any major injuries will require veterinary attention. Keep a suitable carrying box on hand, as you never know when you may need one at short notice. A top-opening cat carrier is ideal.